The Struggle For
DEMOCRACY

The Struggle For
DEMOCRACY

BENJAMIN BARBER
&
PATRICK WATSON

Little, Brown and Company
Boston   Toronto   London

First U.S. Edition

The excerpt from "Easter Uprising" by W.B. Yeats is
reprinted with permission of Macmillan Publishing Company
from *The Poems of W.B. Yeats: A New Edition* edited by
Richard J. Finneran. Copyright © 1924 by Macmillan
Publishing Company, renewed 1952 by Bertha Georgie Yeats.

ISBN: 0-316-08058-6

Library of Congress Catalog Card Number 89-83860

10 9 8 7 6 5 4 3 2 1

RRD OH

Printed in the United States of America

In my thirty-two years of television journalism I have been repeatedly struck by the fact that some of the most corrosive cynicism about democracy and some of the most leaden indifference towards it are expressed by people who live comfortably in prosperous democratic countries. Their own achievements would probably have been impossible without the democratic freedoms they have come to take for granted. Yet I met so many people in the West who were disappointed in their own democratic systems and as a result not contributing to them (or was it the other way around?) that I began to wonder if the story of democracy could be retold in a concentrated and dramatic way – a way that might re-engage the cynics and excite a new generation.

And then, almost twenty years ago, one particular incident helped to galvanize me: in the early predawn of October 16, 1970, police and uniformed officers fanned out across a sleeping city. Armed with extraordinary powers, they broke into homes, ransacked apartments, confiscated what they wanted, and seized people at will; over 450 were arrested. The police had orders to bring in the suspects, and bring in the suspects they did, holding them without charge or bail and refusing to provide reasons for their arrest.

Where did this happen? Not in some remote military dictatorship or totalitarian people's government in Eastern Europe, but in my own country, Canada – one of the world's most peaceable and stable democracies. A shadowy Liberation Front had appeared in Quebec, claiming responsibility for a series of petty "terrorist" incidents and communiqués and for two political kidnappings (one of which would end in a brutal murder). This had panicked and then paralysed Quebec's provincial government and had given the federal

THE MAKING OF THE
TELEVISION SERIES

government a motive for dramatic extra-parliamentary action. Amid rumours of arms caches and insurgents, the government had dusted off an old and half-forgotten legislative bludgeon called the War Measures Act – an act which had last been used to incarcerate Japanese Canadians during the Second World War. Astonishingly, the government's move to suspend civil liberties aroused no significant protest from the Official Opposition, from the press, or from the public at large. Opinion polls taken at the time showed that four out of five Canadians approved of these frightening and wholly undemocratic measures. Canada's much-vaunted commitment to democratic rights and liberties seemed to have vanished overnight.

This casual disowning of freedom – so precious, and so long in the making – troubled me deeply. Hence the television series and the book that accompanies it.

The constricting tragedies in our democratic societies exist cheek by jowl with the liberties and opportunities. A woman said to me in Dublin, where she worked in a women's clinic, "There's no democracy in this bloody country! When they can tell a poor girl she can't have an abortion after she's been gang-raped. When you can't get birth control. When women are treated like slaves." A black American said to me, "There's no democracy in this country, man! Look at the jails. Look at the slums." Again and again I have been confronted – by native people in my own country, by women in almost every democratic country I have visited, by scientists who can't get grants, by victims who see the courts let their assailants go free, by poor people in rich countries, and by rich people enraged at the incursions of the state: millionaires complaining about taxes, and prosperous farmers vilifying marketing boards. Freedoms collide. Over and over I have heard from people hurt in these collisions that there is no democracy, or that it doesn't work, that it is messy and chaotic. "Democracy says that ninety-nine half-wits make a better decision than one man who knows all the facts," said an Australian.

But the struggle for democracy has nevertheless driven the human race for thousands of years. The story of the blood that has been shed to win democratic freedoms is the great ongoing epic in history. There is no civilization that does not bear the mark of democracy; few countries today do not describe themselves by that name. Why?, we asked, as we considered the extraordinary and difficult task of conveying democracy on film. And we began the search for those human stories – stories of self-sacrifice and idealism, of power and invention – that would make sense out of the perplexities of democracy, would celebrate the heroes and heroines of democracy. We set out on a quest for democracy.

In June of 1984 I assembled a panel of scholars and filmmakers to consider how a television series might actually be made on the subject of democracy. Their thoughts propelled me for the next two and a half years – working with as many as three film crews at one time, and filming in some thirty countries. As film came back to Toronto and was processed and screened, the shape of the series, and of this book, began to grow. Early on I met and joined forces with Benjamin Barber, the most satisfying modern thinker about democracy I know, who began as consultant to the series and found himself swept in with us to write the book as well.

I think together we must have accumulated in our travels a total of 500,000 miles. But more striking is the fact that in six months in 1987 I travelled to Britain, Libya, Israel, the United States, Nigeria, Botswana, Zimbabwe, South Africa, Australia, Papua New Guinea, New Zealand, Switzerland, Japan, Holland, Belgium, and France. We were thrown out of Papua New Guinea on a visa technicality and could not get permission to film in South Africa, but in most countries, from Libya to Peru, we found people helpful, if not always easy to deal with. We were especially pleased by the courtesy shown us by armed forces.

Democracy is built upon communication. Television and books both play a vital role in exposing us to the ways of life of people in every part of the globe, to their political aspirations and their personal needs. It is my belief that all this exposure slowly, cumulatively, prepares the ground for accommodations among peoples that will make peace a more achievable objective and democratic forms of social organization inevitable. Not automatically: it will take acts of faith and determination, labours of construction and devising, resources of patience and good will. But it is communication that will both pave the way for these acts and labours and resources, and allow them to become functional. This is the faith of the communicator. It is not a blind faith.

Patrick Watson
Toronto, September 1988

Authors' Acknowledgements

The experience and insight of the many scholars and politicians and the hundreds of citizens and active practitioners of democracy we encountered all over the world are often reflected explicitly in the television series and in these chapters, but there are many wise voices we heard, and learned from, whose wisdom is reflected but not seen. (The opinions and arguments, and the mistakes, are of course our own.)

Our invaluable researcher in New York, Dr. John Samples, made sure that our facts were straight, and provided crucial research and organization of data as well as important bibliographic material. In Canada, Dr. Helen Hatton read the manuscript and drew many historical points to our attention. At Lester & Orpen Dennys, Dean Cooke, Anne Fullerton, and Victoria Foote offered their careful editorial and production assistance, and Louise Dennys, a truly inspiring editor, kept the entire project not just afloat but on an even keel. Juliet Mannock was our indefatigable picture editor. Caroline Furey Bamford not only critically reviewed important sections of the manuscript but took many of the photographs on location. And with his fine sense of design, John Lee gave the book its stamp of distinction and helped stimulate our own imaginations.

But if we were to choose one to whom we would dedicate the book, it would be the late Sir Moses Finley, whose contribution to the study of democratic life and ideas has left a lasting mark on our understanding of western civilization.

Benjamin Barber and Patrick Watson
New York and Toronto, September 1988